CONTENT

Introductions	02
Basketball Great Players	04
Record Breakers	35
Iconic Basketball Teams	68

INTRODUCTIONS

Welcome to the dynamic and exhilarating world of basketball! "100+ Fun Basketball Facts" is your all-access pass to a treasure trove of stories, stats, and facts about one of the most beloved sports on the planet. This book isn't just a collection of data; it's a vibrant journey through the heart and soul of basketball, designed to amaze and inspire both avid fans and curious newcomers alike.

Have you ever wondered about the tallest and shortest players in NBA history and how they played the game? Or perhaps, what makes the strategies of legendary teams so effective? From the hardwood floors of local gyms to the high-stakes buzz of championship games, basketball is a sport rich with extraordinary athletes, mind-blowing records, and heart-pumping moments. Imagine learning about the most nail-biting playoff games, the intricacies of game-winning shots, and the strategic genius of renowned coaches.

So, whether you're a seasoned fan looking to deepen your knowledge or a young enthusiast eager to learn about the magic of basketball, this book is for you. Get ready to immerse yourself in a world where every dribble, dunk, and defensive play tells a story. Let's jump right into the exciting and endless world of basketball!

BASKETBALL GREAT PLAYERS

Michael Jordan's scoring prowess: Michael Jordan, often considered one of the greatest players in NBA history, won 10 scoring titles during his career.

LeBron James' versatility: LeBron James is the only player in NBA history to record over 35,000 points, 9,000 rebounds, and 9,000 assists in his career.

Wilt Chamberlain's 100-point game: Wilt Chamberlain scored a record-breaking 100 points in a single game on March 2, 1962, a feat that has never been matched.

Kareem Abdul-Jabbar's skyhook: Kareem Abdul-Jabbar's iconic skyhook shot was nearly impossible to block and helped him become the NBA's all-time leading scorer.

Larry Bird's three-point accuracy: Larry Bird won three consecutive NBA Three-Point Shootout competitions from 1986 to 1988, showcasing his long-range shooting skills.

Tim Duncan's consistency: Tim Duncan made the NBA All-Defensive First Team and All-NBA Team in the same season for 13 straight years, a record of consistency.

Kobe Bryant's scoring milestones: Kobe Bryant scored 81 points in a single game in 2006, the second-highest point total in a game in NBA history.

Shaquille O'Neal's power and size: Shaquille O'Neal's shoe size is 23, and he famously shattered backboards with his powerful dunks.

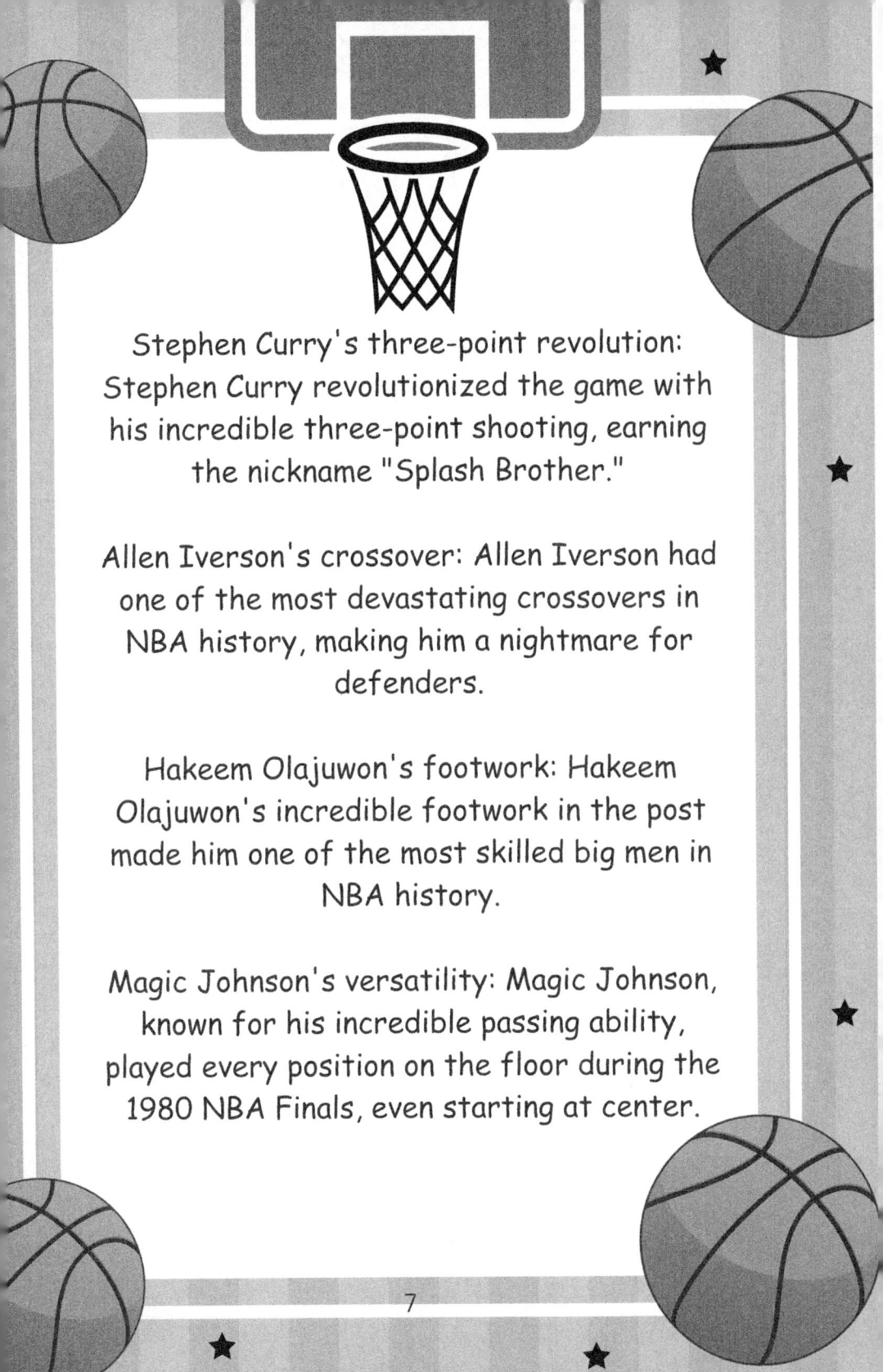

Stephen Curry's three-point revolution: Stephen Curry revolutionized the game with his incredible three-point shooting, earning the nickname "Splash Brother."

Allen Iverson's crossover: Allen Iverson had one of the most devastating crossovers in NBA history, making him a nightmare for defenders.

Hakeem Olajuwon's footwork: Hakeem Olajuwon's incredible footwork in the post made him one of the most skilled big men in NBA history.

Magic Johnson's versatility: Magic Johnson, known for his incredible passing ability, played every position on the floor during the 1980 NBA Finals, even starting at center.

Bill Russell's championship dominance: Bill Russell won an astounding 11 NBA championships with the Boston Celtics, the most by any player in NBA history.

Vince Carter's dunking prowess: Vince Carter's slam dunks, especially his iconic 2000 Olympics "Dunk of Death," made him a fan favorite.

Karl Malone's durability: Karl Malone, known as "The Mailman," played 1,476 games in his NBA career, the second-most in league history.

Kevin Durant's scoring efficiency: Kevin Durant has led the league in scoring multiple times while maintaining an impressive shooting percentage.

Tim Duncan's consistency: Tim Duncan is the only player in NBA history to win over 1,000 games with a single team, the San Antonio Spurs.

Larry Bird's three consecutive MVP awards: Larry Bird is one of only three players in NBA history to win three consecutive Most Valuable Player (MVP) awards.

Wilt Chamberlain's 50-point games: Wilt Chamberlain holds the record for the most 50-point games in a season, with 45 such games in the 1961-62 season.

John Stockton's assists: John Stockton holds the record for the most career assists in NBA history, with 15,806 assists during his career.

Scottie Pippen's versatility: Scottie Pippen is the only player in NBA history to record over 200 steals and 100 blocked shots in a single season.

Dennis Rodman's rebounding: Dennis Rodman led the NBA in rebounds for seven consecutive seasons, and he once averaged 18.7 rebounds per game in a season.

Steve Nash's assists and shooting: Steve Nash won the NBA Most Valuable Player (MVP) award twice and is one of the most accurate free-throw and three-point shooters in NBA history.

Kawhi Leonard's defensive prowess: Kawhi Leonard is known for his defensive skills and has won multiple NBA Defensive Player of the Year awards.

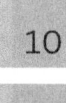

Kevin Garnett's intensity: Kevin Garnett was known for his intense on-court demeanor and is one of the few players to have accumulated over 25,000 points, 10,000 rebounds, 5,000 assists, and 1,500 steals in his career.

Chris Paul's assists and steals: Chris Paul is one of the league's all-time leaders in assists and steals and has consistently been among the top point guards in the NBA.

Carmelo Anthony's scoring: Carmelo Anthony is one of the most prolific scorers in NBA history, with over 27,000 career points.

Paul Pierce's clutch performances: Paul Pierce earned the nickname "The Truth" for his ability to perform exceptionally well in crucial moments during games.

Yao Ming's impact: Yao Ming, a former NBA player from China, played a significant role in popularizing basketball in Asia and fostering international talent.

Hakeem Olajuwon's footwork: Hakeem Olajuwon's impeccable footwork and post moves made him one of the most skilled centers in NBA history.

Karl Malone and John Stockton's partnership: Karl Malone and John Stockton formed one of the most successful duos in NBA history, collectively achieving numerous records and accolades.

Allen Iverson's fearless play: Despite his small stature, Allen Iverson was known for his incredible scoring ability and tenacity on the court.

Dirk Nowitzki's loyalty: Dirk Nowitzki spent his entire 21-season NBA career with the Dallas Mavericks, becoming one of the greatest power forwards in history.

Karl Malone's durability: Karl Malone, known as "The Mailman," played in 1,476 regular-season games, the second-most in NBA history.

Vince Carter's longevity: Vince Carter played in the NBA for 22 seasons, making him one of the longest-tenured players in league history.

Magic Johnson's versatility: Magic Johnson is the only player in NBA Finals history to record a triple-double in his rookie season.

Michael Jordan's comeback: Michael Jordan retired from basketball twice but returned both times to win NBA championships with the Chicago Bulls.

LeBron James' triple-doubles: LeBron James has the most triple-doubles in NBA playoff history, showcasing his all-around skills.

Bill Russell's championship dominance: Bill Russell won an astonishing 11 NBA championships in his 13-year career with the Boston Celtics.

Charles Barkley's rebounding ability: Charles Barkley, despite being undersized for a power forward, was one of the best rebounders in NBA history.

Dirk Nowitzki's one-legged fadeaway: Dirk Nowitzki's signature move, the one-legged fadeaway, was nearly impossible to defend.

Hakeem Olajuwon's quadruple-double: Hakeem Olajuwon is one of only four players in NBA history to record a quadruple-double, achieving this feat in 1990.

Kevin Durant's scoring efficiency: Kevin Durant is known for his scoring prowess and is one of the few players to have won multiple NBA scoring titles.

Charles Barkley's rebounding ability: Charles Barkley, despite being undersized for a power forward, was one of the best rebounders in NBA history.

Dirk Nowitzki's one-legged fadeaway: Dirk Nowitzki's signature move, the one-legged fadeaway, was nearly impossible to defend.

Hakeem Olajuwon's quadruple-double: Hakeem Olajuwon is one of only four players in NBA history to record a quadruple-double, achieving this feat in 1990.

Kevin Durant's scoring efficiency: Kevin Durant is known for his scoring prowess and is one of the few players to have won multiple NBA scoring titles.

Shaquille O'Neal's dunking power: Shaquille O'Neal broke multiple backboards during his career due to his powerful dunks, leading to the NBA changing the design of its backboards.

George Mikan's impact: George Mikan, one of the pioneers of professional basketball, introduced the concept of shot-blocking as a dominant center in the 1940s and 1950s.

Oscar Robertson's triple-doubles: Oscar Robertson is the only player in NBA history to average a triple-double for an entire season, accomplishing this feat in the 1961-62 season.

Reggie Miller's clutch shooting: Reggie Miller was known for his ability to make crucial three-point shots during high-pressure moments in games, earning him the nickname "Knick Killer."

Elgin Baylor's scoring ability: Elgin Baylor once scored 71 points in a single game, which was the second-highest point total in a single game at that time.

Bob Cousy's playmaking: Bob Cousy was known for his exceptional ball-handling and passing skills, revolutionizing the point guard position in basketball.

Jerry West's logo: The NBA's iconic silhouette logo, featuring a player dribbling a basketball, is based on Hall of Famer Jerry West.

David Robinson's character: David Robinson, known as the "Admiral," was not only a dominant player but also a respected leader both on and off the court.

Moses Malone's work ethic: Moses Malone famously predicted that the Philadelphia 76ers would win the NBA championship in 1983, and they did. He was known for his relentless work ethic and rebounding prowess.

Isiah Thomas' leadership: Isiah Thomas was a fearless leader and the driving force behind the Detroit Pistons' "Bad Boys" era, winning two NBA championships.

Tracy McGrady's scoring bursts: Tracy McGrady once scored 13 points in the final 35 seconds of a game to lead the Houston Rockets to an incredible comeback victory.

Dwyane Wade's Finals MVP: Dwyane Wade's performance in the 2006 NBA Finals, where he averaged 34.7 points per game, earned him the Finals MVP award.

Chris Bosh's versatility: Chris Bosh transitioned from a dominant post player to a sharpshooting forward when he joined the Miami Heat's "Big Three" alongside LeBron James and Dwyane Wade.

Kareem Abdul-Jabbar's longevity: Kareem Abdul-Jabbar played in the NBA for 20 seasons, retiring as the all-time leading scorer with 38,387 points.

Kevin Garnett's intensity: Kevin Garnett was known for his fierce competitiveness and his famous "Anything is possible!" exclamation after winning the NBA championship with the Boston Celtics.

Kawhi Leonard's Finals MVP awards: Kawhi Leonard is the only player in NBA history to have won NBA Finals MVP with two different teams (San Antonio Spurs and Toronto Raptors).

Bill Russell's defensive prowess: Bill Russell was a dominant shot-blocker and defender, leading the NBA in blocked shots during four seasons.

Allen Iverson's scoring titles: Allen Iverson led the league in scoring four times during his career, despite his relatively small stature for an NBA player.

Charles Barkley's versatility: Charles Barkley is the shortest player in NBA history to lead the league in rebounds, standing at 6 feet 6 inches tall.

Elvin Hayes' durability: Elvin Hayes played in 1,303 consecutive games, showcasing remarkable durability throughout his career.

George Gervin's scoring prowess: George Gervin was known as the "Iceman" and led the league in scoring four times during his career.

Nate Thurmond's quadruple-double: Nate Thurmond recorded one of only four quadruple-doubles in NBA history with 22 points, 14 rebounds, 13 assists, and 12 blocks in a single game.

Walt Chamberlain's records: Wilt Chamberlain holds numerous records, including the highest single-season scoring average (50.4 points per game) and the most rebounds in a single game (55).

Jason Kidd's triple-doubles: Jason Kidd ranks second on the all-time triple-doubles list, showcasing his remarkable ability to contribute in points, rebounds, and assists.

James Harden's scoring records: James Harden holds the record for the most points scored in a single season without scoring 50 or more points in a single game.

Dominique Wilkins' dunking ability: Dominique Wilkins was a high-flying dunker and won the NBA Slam Dunk Contest twice.

Dominique Wilkins: Dominique Wilkins, known for his high-flying dunks, won two NBA Slam Dunk Contests and was a nine-time NBA All-Star.

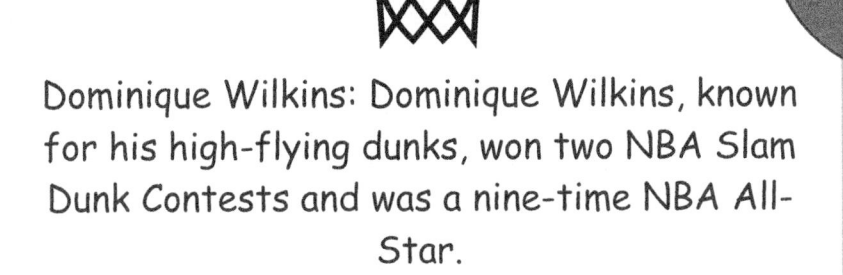

Reggie Miller: Reggie Miller is one of the greatest clutch shooters in NBA history and is known for his memorable moments in pressure situations, including his eight points in nine seconds during a playoff game.

Michael Jordan: Michael Jordan is the only player to win the NBA Most Valuable Player (MVP) and NBA Finals MVP in the same season five times.

Kareem Abdul-Jabbar: Kareem Abdul-Jabbar, known for his skyhook shot, scored more points with that one signature move than any other player scored with a single shot in NBA history.

Magic Johnson: Magic Johnson recorded a triple-double in his NBA Finals debut as a rookie, solidifying his reputation as one of the greatest point guards ever.

Larry Bird: Larry Bird won three consecutive NBA Most Valuable Player (MVP) awards from 1984 to 1986, becoming the only player in NBA history to achieve this feat.

Tim Duncan: Tim Duncan is the only player in NBA history to start and win an NBA Finals game in three different decades (1990s, 2000s, 2010s).

Shaquille O'Neal: Shaquille O'Neal was so dominant in the paint that the NBA implemented the "Hack-a-Shaq" strategy, intentionally fouling him to send him to the free-throw line, where he struggled

Hakeem Olajuwon: Hakeem Olajuwon is the only player in NBA history to record over 2,000 career blocks and over 2,000 career steals.

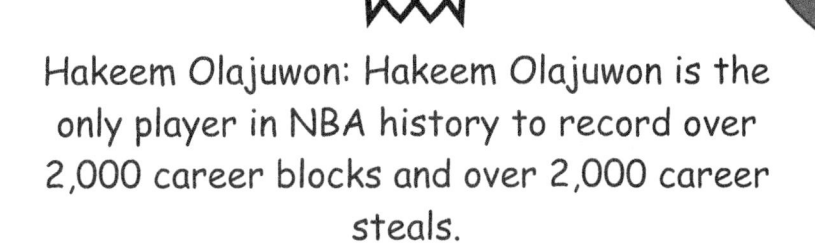

Wilt Chamberlain: Wilt Chamberlain once averaged 50.4 points per game in a single season, the highest scoring average in NBA history.

Bill Russell: Bill Russell won 11 NBA championships in his 13-year career, cementing his legacy as one of the most successful players in sports history.

Dirk Nowitzki: Dirk Nowitzki is the only player in NBA history to record over 30,000 points, 10,000 rebounds, and 1,000 three-pointers in his career as a 7-footer.

Karl Malone: Karl Malone, known as "The Mailman," was a two-time NBA MVP and the second-leading scorer in NBA history with 36,928 points.

Jerry West: Jerry West is the only player to win the NBA Finals MVP award while playing for the losing team. He achieved this in 1969 when his Los Angeles Lakers lost to the Boston Celtics in the NBA Finals.

Isiah Thomas: Isiah Thomas, a Hall of Fame point guard, once played an entire NBA Finals game with a severe ankle injury, demonstrating his toughness and determination.

Oscar Robertson: Oscar Robertson is the only player in NBA history to average a triple-double for an entire season. He achieved this remarkable feat during the 1961-1962 season.

Charles Barkley: Charles Barkley, despite being known for his rebounding prowess, never had a 20-rebound game during his NBA career.

Allen Iverson: Allen Iverson, a prolific scorer, led the league in points per game for four seasons and is the shortest player (6'0") to win the NBA scoring title.

Dwyane Wade: Dwyane Wade is the only player in NBA history to record at least 2,000 points, 500 assists, 100 steals, and 100 blocks in a single season, which he accomplished during the 2008-2009 season.

Elgin Baylor: Elgin Baylor scored an incredible 61 points in an NBA Finals game in 1962, a record that still stands as the most points scored in a Finals game.

George Gervin: George Gervin, known as the "Iceman," once scored 33 points in a single quarter, a feat that showcases his scoring ability.

Kawhi Leonard: Kawhi Leonard has won NBA Finals MVP with two different teams, the San Antonio Spurs and the Toronto Raptors, a testament to his impact on the championship stage.

Dennis Rodman's Rebounding Dominance: Dennis Rodman led the NBA in rebounding for seven consecutive seasons, showcasing his extraordinary skills as a rebounder.

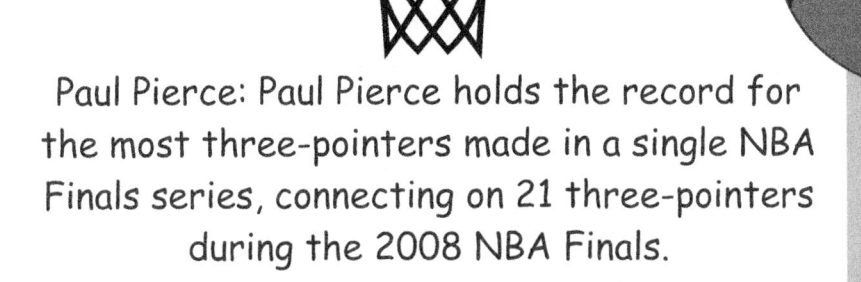

Paul Pierce: Paul Pierce holds the record for the most three-pointers made in a single NBA Finals series, connecting on 21 three-pointers during the 2008 NBA Finals.

Chris Paul: Chris Paul leads the NBA in career assists per game and steals per game among active players, showcasing his playmaking and defensive prowess.

Carmelo Anthony: Carmelo Anthony is one of the most prolific scorers in NBA history and ranks in the top 10 for career points scored.

Steve Nash: Steve Nash, a two-time NBA MVP, is one of the greatest point guards in history and is known for his exceptional passing ability. He led the league in assists for five seasons.

Hakeem Olajuwon's Quadruple-Double: Hakeem Olajuwon recorded a quadruple-double in 1990, becoming the only player in NBA history to achieve this feat with 18 points, 16 rebounds, 10 assists, and 11 blocks in a single game.

Tracy McGrady's Scoring Outbursts: Tracy McGrady once scored 13 points in the final 35 seconds of a game to lead his team to a remarkable comeback victory.

Pau Gasol and Marc Gasol: Pau and Marc Gasol are the only brothers to win NBA championships, with Pau winning two titles with the Los Angeles Lakers and Marc winning one with the Toronto Raptors.

Allen Iverson's Rookie of the Year and MVP: Allen Iverson is the only player to win both the NBA Rookie of the Year and MVP awards in the same season (1996-1997).

Reggie Miller's Three-Point Milestones: Reggie Miller retired as the NBA's all-time leader in three-pointers made and was known for his clutch three-point shooting in the playoffs.

Walt Chamberlain's 100-Point Game: Wilt Chamberlain scored a historic 100 points in a single game in 1962, a record that still stands as the highest-scoring game in NBA history.

George Mikan's Dominance: George Mikan, one of the pioneers of the NBA, was so dominant that the league introduced the shot clock to counter his scoring and shot-blocking abilities.

Karl Malone's Durability: Karl Malone played 1,476 regular-season games in his career, an NBA record for most games played, showcasing his incredible durability.

Chris Webber's Historic Rookie Season: Chris Webber had an exceptional rookie season and became the only player to record over 20 points, 9 rebounds, and 4 assists per game as a rookie.

Rick Barry's Free-Throw Shooting: Rick Barry, known for his underhanded free-throw shooting style, retired as one of the most accurate free-throw shooters in NBA history.

RECORD BREAKERS

Triple-Double Records: A triple-double occurs when a player records double digits in three statistical categories (usually points, rebounds, and assists). The player with the most career triple-doubles in NBA history is Oscar Robertson, with 181.

50-Point Games: Scoring 50 or more points in a single game is a remarkable feat. Wilt Chamberlain holds the record for the most 50-point games in a single season, with 45 in the 1961-62 season.

Most Points in a Game: Wilt Chamberlain also holds the record for the most points scored in a single game, with 100 points in a game played on March 2, 1962.

Three-Point Records: Stephen Curry is the all-time leader in three-pointers made in both regular-season and playoff games. He has revolutionized the game with his long-range shooting.

Free Throw Percentage: Steve Nash holds the record for the highest career free throw percentage in NBA history, with an accuracy rate of 90.43%.

Consecutive Free Throws Made: The record for consecutive free throws made in an NBA game belongs to Damian Lillard, who made 64 consecutive free throws during the 2020-2021 season.

Fastest Triple-Double: Russell Westbrook holds the record for the fastest triple-double in NBA history, achieving one in just 21 minutes of play during a game in 2016.

Unbreakable Records: Some records, such as Wilt Chamberlain's 100-point game and his season average of 50.4 points per game, are often considered nearly impossible to break in the modern NBA.

Shooting Percentage Records: Players like DeAndre Jordan and Wilt Chamberlain have achieved seasons with field goal percentages well above 70%, showcasing their efficiency near the basket.

Fastest Triple-Double: Russell Westbrook holds the record for the fastest triple-double in NBA history, achieving one in just 21 minutes of play during a game in 2016.

Unbreakable Records: Some records, such as Wilt Chamberlain's 100-point game and his season average of 50.4 points per game, are often considered nearly impossible to break in the modern NBA.

Shooting Percentage Records: Players like DeAndre Jordan and Wilt Chamberlain have achieved seasons with field goal percentages well above 70%, showcasing their efficiency near the basket.

Steals and Blocks Records: John Stockton holds the record for the most career steals, while Hakeem Olajuwon is the all-time leader in career blocks.

Minutes Played: Kareem Abdul-Jabbar holds the record for the most career minutes played in the NBA, with over 57,000 minutes.

Scoring Titles: Michael Jordan won the most scoring titles in NBA history, with 10, highlighting his incredible scoring ability.

Assists Records: John Stockton is the all-time leader in career assists and assists per game, averaging 10.5 assists over his career.

Quadruple-Double Rarity: Quadruple-doubles, where a player records double digits in four statistical categories (typically points, rebounds, assists, and blocks or steals), are extremely rare. Only four quadruple-doubles have been officially recorded in NBA history.

Highest Scoring Game: The highest-scoring game in NBA history took place on December 13, 1983, between the Detroit Pistons and the Denver Nuggets. The final score was 186-184 in triple overtime, with the Pistons winning.

Most Assists in a Game: Scott Skiles holds the record for the most assists in a single game, with 30 assists in a game played on December 30, 1990, when he played for the Orlando Magic.

Longest Winning Streak: The longest winning streak in NBA history belongs to the 1971-72 Los Angeles Lakers, who won 33 consecutive games during the regular season.

Most Three-Pointers in a Game: Klay Thompson holds the record for the most three-pointers made in a single game, with 14 three-pointers in a game played on October 29, 2018.

Perfect Shooting Game: Wilt Chamberlain holds the record for the most points scored in a game without missing a field goal attempt. He scored 36 points on 100% shooting (18-18) on February 24, 1967.

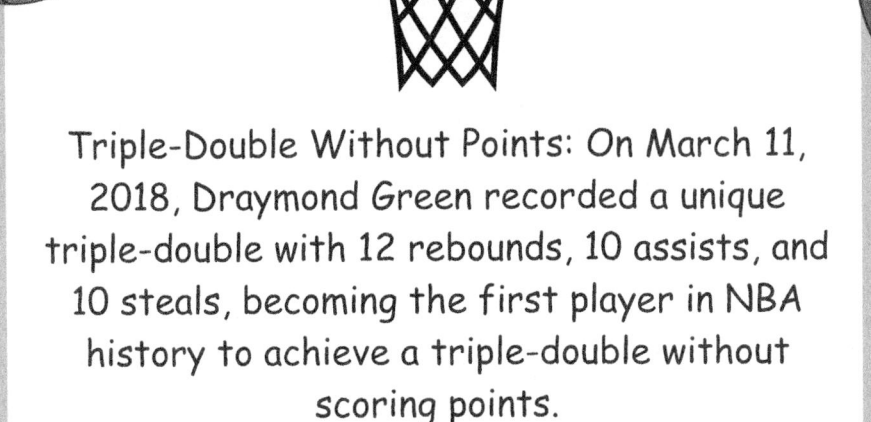

Triple-Double Without Points: On March 11, 2018, Draymond Green recorded a unique triple-double with 12 rebounds, 10 assists, and 10 steals, becoming the first player in NBA history to achieve a triple-double without scoring points.

Youngest MVP: Derrick Rose became the youngest player in NBA history to win the Most Valuable Player (MVP) award when he earned the honor at the age of 22 in 2011.

Most Consecutive Games Played: A.C. Green holds the record for the most consecutive games played in the NBA, with 1,192 consecutive games played during his career.

Career Triple-Doubles: LeBron James is one of the few players who have recorded triple-doubles against every NBA team during his career.

Perfect Free Throw Shooting: José Calderón set the record for the highest single-season free throw percentage, making 98.1% of his free throws during the 2008-2009 season.

Oldest Player: Vince Carter holds the record for being the oldest player to record a triple-double in an NBA game, achieving the feat at 42 years and 37 days old.

Perfect Three-Point Shooting Game: On January 15, 2007, Gilbert Arenas of the Washington Wizards made all eight of his three-point attempts in a game against the Phoenix Suns, setting an NBA record for the most three-pointers without a miss in a single game.

Fastest Triple-Double in Minutes: Jim Tucker of the Syracuse Nationals recorded the fastest triple-double in NBA history. He achieved it in just 17 minutes of playing time on February 20, 1955.

NBA's Youngest Player: Andrew Bynum became the youngest player ever to play in an NBA game when he made his debut for the Los Angeles Lakers at the age of 18 years and 6 days.

Most Points Scored in a Quarter: Klay Thompson set an NBA record by scoring 37 points in a single quarter during a game on January 23, 2015, for the Golden State Warriors.

Highest Career Scoring Average: Michael Jordan holds the highest career scoring average in NBA history, averaging 30.1 points per game over his career.

Most Career Blocks for a Guard: Dwyane Wade, primarily known for his scoring and playmaking, ranks among the top guards in NBA history in terms of career blocks.

Larry Bird's Free Throw Accuracy: Larry Bird led the NBA in free throw percentage for four consecutive seasons, making him one of the most accurate free throw shooters in history.

Youngest Player to Reach 30,000 Points: LeBron James became the youngest player to reach 30,000 career points in the NBA at the age of 33 years and 24 days.

Most Three-Pointers Made in a Season: Stephen Curry shattered his own record for the most three-pointers made in a single season multiple times, establishing a new benchmark for long-range shooting.

Most Triple-Doubles in a Season: Russell Westbrook set the record for the most triple-doubles in a single season, recording 42 during the 2016-2017 season.

Most Career Rebounds for a Guard: Jason Kidd, known for his exceptional passing, ranks among the top guards in NBA history in terms of career rebounds.

Longest Game in NBA History: The longest NBA game in history took place on January 6, 1951, when the Indianapolis Olympians defeated the Rochester Royals 75-73 in six overtimes.

Most Points in a Playoff Game: Michael Jordan holds the record for the most points scored in a single NBA playoff game with 63 points, achieved in a game against the Boston Celtics in 1986.

Most Assists in a Playoff Game: John Stockton recorded the most assists in a single NBA playoff game with 24 assists during a game in 1988.

Longest Winning Streak in a Single Season: The 2015-2016 Golden State Warriors won 24 consecutive games in a single season, tying the record for the longest winning streak.

Highest Scoring Playoff Game: The highest-scoring NBA playoff game took place on April 24, 1984, when the Denver Nuggets defeated the San Antonio Spurs 163-155 in triple overtime.

Most Consecutive Free Throws Made: José Calderón holds the NBA record for the most consecutive free throws made in a single season, with 98 consecutive successful attempts in the 2008-2009 season.

Most Blocked Shots in a Game: Elmore Smith recorded 17 blocked shots in a single NBA game in 1973, setting the record for the most blocks in a game.

Most Three-Pointers in a Playoff Game: Donovan Mitchell set the record for the most three-pointers made in a single NBA playoff game with 11 three-pointers in 2021.

Most Steals in a Single Season: Alvin Robertson holds the record for the most steals in a single NBA season, with 301 steals during the 1985-1986 season.

Youngest Player to Score 50 Points: Devin Booker became the youngest player in NBA history to score 50 or more points in a game when he achieved this feat at the age of 20 years and 145 days.

Highest Career Free Throw Percentage (Active Player): Stephen Curry has the highest career free throw percentage among active NBA players, consistently maintaining a high accuracy rate.

Most Points in a Playoff Series: Michael Jordan holds the record for the most points scored in a single NBA playoff series, with 246 points in a six-game series against the Cleveland Cavaliers in 1988.

Most Points in an NBA Debut: Wilt Chamberlain scored 43 points in his NBA debut in 1959, setting a record for the most points scored by a rookie in their first game.

Youngest NBA Coach: At the age of 27, Kevin Garnett became the youngest head coach in NBA history when he took on the role of player-coach for the Minnesota Timberwolves in 2021.

Most Three-Pointers Made in a Career: Ray Allen holds the record for the most three-pointers made in an NBA career, with 2,973 made three-pointers.

Most Blocks in a Single Game: Elmore Smith and Manute Bol share the record for the most blocks in a single NBA game with 17 blocked shots.

Longest Uninterrupted Triple-Double Streak: Russell Westbrook recorded a triple-double in 11 consecutive games during the 2018-2019 season, setting a new NBA record.

Most Points in an Overtime Game: Gilbert Arenas scored 60 points in a game against the Los Angeles Lakers in 2006, setting the record for the most points scored in an overtime game.

Most Three-Pointers in a Single Playoff Run: Stephen Curry holds the record for the most three-pointers made in a single NBA playoff run, with 98 three-pointers during the 2015 playoffs.

Most Points in a Single Half: Klay Thompson scored 37 points in a single half during a game in 2015, setting an NBA record for the most points in a half.

Highest Scoring NBA Finals Game: Game 5 of the 1976 NBA Finals between the Boston Celtics and Phoenix Suns went into triple overtime, with both teams scoring 128 points, making it the highest-scoring NBA Finals game.

Most Wins in a Regular Season: The 2015-2016 Golden State Warriors hold the record for the most wins in a single NBA regular season, with 73 wins and 9 losses.

Most Consecutive Playoff Appearances: The San Antonio Spurs set a record by making the playoffs for 22 consecutive seasons from 1998 to 2019.

Highest Career Points Per Game Average: Elgin Baylor has the highest career points per game average in NBA Finals history, averaging 34.04 points per game.

Most Assists in a Game by a Rookie: Ernie DiGregorio recorded 25 assists in a single game as a rookie for the Buffalo Braves in 1974, setting a record for most assists in a game by a rookie.

Most Points in a Single Quarter: George Gervin scored 33 points in a single quarter during a game in 1978, setting the record for the most points scored in a quarter.

Most Career Assists for a Forward: LeBron James, primarily known as a forward, ranks among the top players in NBA history in terms of career assists.

Highest Single-Season Assist Average: John Stockton holds the record for the highest single-season assist average, with 14.5 assists per game during the 1989-1990 season.

Most Triple-Doubles in a Calendar Month: Russell Westbrook holds the record for the most triple-doubles in a calendar month, recording 20 in the month of March 2017.

Most Points in a Playoff Series: LeBron James scored 216 points in a six-game playoff series against the Boston Celtics in 2012, setting a record for the most points in a playoff series.

Most Points Scored in an NBA All-Star Game: Wilt Chamberlain scored 42 points in the 1962 NBA All-Star Game, setting the record for the most points scored in an All-Star Game.

Highest Career Field Goal Percentage: Artis Gilmore holds the record for the highest career field goal percentage in NBA history, with a career shooting percentage of 59.9%.

Most Consecutive Games with a Three-Pointer Made: Stephen Curry holds the record for the most consecutive games with at least one three-pointer made, with a streak that lasted for 157 games.

Most Career Rebounds for a Guard (Active Player): Russell Westbrook is among the top guards in NBA history in terms of career rebounds, ranking high in this category among active players.

Most Points Scored in a Game by a Rookie: Wilt Chamberlain holds the record for the most points scored by a rookie in a single game, with 58 points in a game in 1960.

Most Assists in a Single Playoff Game: John Stockton recorded 24 assists in a single NBA playoff game, setting a record for the most assists in a playoff game.

Most Three-Pointers Made in a Single Playoff Run (Team): The 2017-2018 Golden State Warriors set a record for the most three-pointers made by a team in a single playoff run, with 312 three-pointers made during the postseason.

Highest Career Scoring Average for a Rookie: Wilt Chamberlain holds the record for the highest career scoring average for a rookie, averaging 37.6 points per game in his rookie season.

Most Points in a Playoff Series (Team): The 1982 Denver Nuggets hold the record for the most points scored by a team in a single playoff series, accumulating 1,046 points in a first-round series against the San Antonio Spurs.

Highest Career Scoring Average in the Playoffs: Michael Jordan has the highest career scoring average in NBA playoff history, averaging 33.4 points per game during his postseason career.

Most Assists in an NBA Finals Game: Magic Johnson recorded 21 assists in a single NBA Finals game, setting a record for the most assists in an NBA Finals game.

Most Points in an NBA Finals Game (Non-Overtime): Elgin Baylor scored 61 points in an NBA Finals game in 1962, setting the record for the most points scored in a Finals game without going into overtime.

Most Three-Pointers Made in an NBA Finals Series: Ray Allen made 22 three-pointers in the 2013 NBA Finals series, setting a record for the most three-pointers made in a Finals series.

Most Career Playoff Points: LeBron James holds the record for the most career playoff points in NBA history, surpassing Michael Jordan's previous record.

Highest Career Playoff Rebound Average: Bill Russell has the highest career playoff rebound average in NBA history, averaging 24.9 rebounds per game in the postseason.

Highest Career Playoff Block Average: Hakeem Olajuwon has the highest career playoff block average, averaging 3.3 blocks per game in the postseason.

Highest Single-Game Scoring Averages: Wilt Chamberlain averaged 50.4 points per game during the 1961-1962 season, setting a record for the highest single-season scoring average. He also had a season where he averaged 48.5 points per game.

Highest Scoring NBA Finals Game (Overtime): Rick Barry scored 55 points in an NBA Finals game in 1967, which went into overtime, setting the record for the most points in a Finals game that included overtime.

Most Three-Pointers in a Season (Team): The 2018-2019 Houston Rockets hold the record for the most three-pointers made by a team in a single season, with 1,323 three-pointers made during the regular season.

Most Consecutive Games Played (Including Playoffs): A.C. Green played in 1,192 consecutive games, including regular-season and playoff games, setting a remarkable durability record.

Most Assists in a Single Game (Playoffs): John Stockton holds the record for the most assists in a single playoff game, with 24 assists during a game in the 1988 NBA playoffs.

Most Three-Pointers in a Single NBA Game (Individual): Klay Thompson set the record for the most three-pointers made by a player in a single NBA game with 14 three-pointers on October 29, 2018.

Most Three-Pointers in a Single Playoff Game (Team): The Golden State Warriors made 27 three-pointers in a single playoff game in 2019, setting the record for the most three-pointers by a team in a playoff game.

Most Career Points Off the Bench: Jamal Crawford is the all-time leader in career points scored as a reserve, demonstrating his scoring ability coming off the bench.

Most Career Triple-Doubles in NBA Playoffs: LeBron James holds the record for the most career triple-doubles in NBA playoff history, showcasing his versatility in postseason play.

Highest Single-Game Rebound Average (Regular Season): Wilt Chamberlain averaged a staggering 27.2 rebounds per game during the 1960-1961 NBA season.

Most Assists in an NBA Season (Individual): John Stockton set the record for the most assists in a single NBA season, with 1,164 assists during the 1989-1990 season.

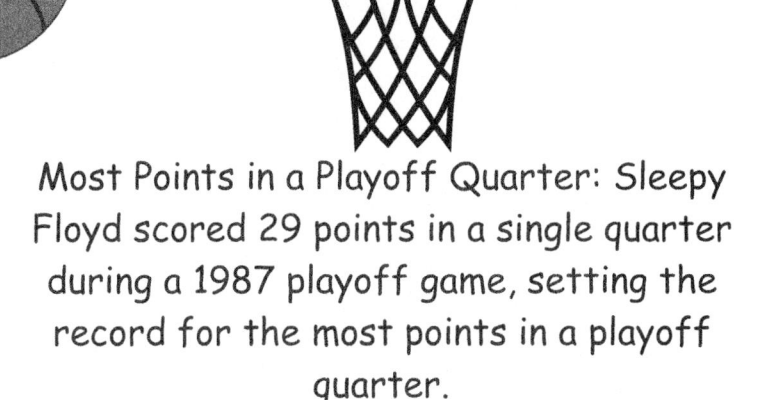

Most Points in a Playoff Quarter: Sleepy Floyd scored 29 points in a single quarter during a 1987 playoff game, setting the record for the most points in a playoff quarter.

Highest Career Three-Point Percentage (Active Player): Stephen Curry has the highest career three-point shooting percentage among active NBA players.

Most Three-Pointers Made in a Single Playoff Run (Individual): Stephen Curry set a record by making 98 three-pointers in a single postseason run in 2015.

Highest Single-Game Steals Average (Playoffs): Allen Iverson recorded 10 steals in a single playoff game, showcasing his defensive prowess.

Most Points in an NBA All-Star Game (Individual): Wilt Chamberlain scored 42 points in an NBA All-Star Game, setting the record for the most points scored by a player in an All-Star Game.

Most Triple-Doubles in a Single NBA Season (Team): The 1981-1982 Milwaukee Bucks set the record for the most triple-doubles by a team in a single NBA season, with 35 triple-doubles.

Most Points in an NBA Finals Game (Regulation): Elgin Baylor scored 61 points in a regulation NBA Finals game in 1962, setting the record for the most points in an NBA Finals game without overtime.

Most Three-Pointers Made in a Single NBA Finals Series (Individual): Stephen Curry set a record by making 32 three-pointers in a single NBA Finals series in 2018.

Most Points in a Single Playoff Run (Team): The 2018 Golden State Warriors scored a record 3,355 points in a single playoff run.

Highest Average Points Per Game in a Single Playoff Run (Individual): Michael Jordan averaged 43.7 points per game during the 1986 NBA playoffs, setting a record for the highest points per game average in a single postseason run.

Most Consecutive Triple-Doubles (Playoffs): Magic Johnson recorded a triple-double in eight consecutive playoff games, showcasing his postseason brilliance.

Most Points in an NBA All-Star Game Half (Individual): Glen Rice scored 20 points in a single half during an NBA All-Star Game, setting the record for the most points in a half.

Most Three-Pointers Made in a Single Season (Team): The 2017-2018 Houston Rockets set a record for the most three-pointers made by a team in a single regular season with 1,256 three-pointers.

Most Points in a Single Playoff Series (Individual): Michael Jordan averaged 45.2 points per game in a six-game playoff series against the Boston Celtics in 1986, setting a record for the most points in a single playoff series.

Most Career Points Scored in the NBA: Karl Malone is second on the all-time career points list in the NBA, with 36,928 points.

Highest Single-Game Rebound Average (Playoffs): Bill Russell averaged 40.5 rebounds per game in a single playoff series in 1960, setting a remarkable record.

Most Consecutive Triple-Doubles (Regular Season): Russell Westbrook recorded a triple-double in 11 consecutive regular-season games during the 2018-2019 season, tying the record.

Most Career Points in NBA History: Kareem Abdul-Jabbar is the all-time leading scorer in NBA history, with 38,387 career points.

ICONIC BASKETBALL TEAMS

Boston Celtics' Championships: The Boston Celtics hold the record for the most NBA championships, with 17 titles to their name.

Los Angeles Lakers' Dominance: The Los Angeles Lakers have appeared in the NBA Finals 32 times and have won 17 championships, tying them with the Boston Celtics for the most titles.

Chicago Bulls' Historic Season: The Chicago Bulls set a regular-season record with 72 wins and only 10 losses during the 1995-1996 season, a record that stood for over two decades.

San Antonio Spurs' Consistency: The San Antonio Spurs have made the playoffs for 22 consecutive seasons, showcasing remarkable consistency and success.

Golden State Warriors' Three-Point Revolution: The Golden State Warriors set an NBA record for the most three-pointers made in a single season, a record they broke multiple times during their championship runs.

Philadelphia 76ers' Win Streak: The 1971-1972 Philadelphia 76ers hold the record for the longest winning streak in NBA history, with 33 consecutive wins.

Oklahoma City Thunder's Quick Rise: The Oklahoma City Thunder, formerly the Seattle SuperSonics, made the NBA Finals in just their fourth season after relocating to Oklahoma City.

Los Angeles Clippers' Turnaround: The Los Angeles Clippers, historically one of the NBA's least successful franchises, have experienced a resurgence in recent years, becoming playoff contenders.

Milwaukee Bucks' Record Regular Season: The Milwaukee Bucks had one of the best regular seasons in NBA history in 1971 when they finished with a 66-16 record.

Portland Trail Blazers' Iconic Draft: The Portland Trail Blazers selected Bill Walton with the first overall pick in the 1974 NBA Draft, and he went on to lead the team to an NBA championship in 1977.

Utah Jazz's Consistent Playoff Appearances: The Utah Jazz made the playoffs for 20 consecutive seasons from 1984 to 2003, establishing themselves as a perennial contender.

Miami Heat's "Big Three": The Miami Heat formed a "Big Three" of LeBron James, Dwyane Wade, and Chris Bosh in 2010, leading the team to four consecutive NBA Finals appearances and two championships.

Phoenix Suns' Fast-Paced Style: The Phoenix Suns, under coach Mike D'Antoni, popularized a fast-paced style of play known as "Seven Seconds or Less," emphasizing quick possessions and three-point shooting.

Houston Rockets' Triple-Double Streak: The Houston Rockets set an NBA record with 27 consecutive games with at least one three-pointer made, showcasing their reliance on the long-range shot.

New York Knicks' Historic Seasons: The New York Knicks have had several historic seasons, including the 1969-1970 season when they won their first NBA championship and the 1993-1994 season when they reached the NBA Finals.

Dallas Mavericks' Championship Run: The Dallas Mavericks won their first NBA championship in the 2010-2011 season, led by Dirk Nowitzki and defeating the Miami Heat in the NBA Finals.

Atlanta Hawks' Dominance in the 1960s: The St. Louis Hawks, which later became the Atlanta Hawks, were a dominant force in the early 1960s, reaching the NBA Finals four times in a row from 1957 to 1960 and winning the championship in 1958.

Detroit Pistons' "Bad Boys" Era: The Detroit Pistons, known as the "Bad Boys" in the late 1980s and early 1990s, were known for their physical style of play and won back-to-back NBA championships in 1989 and 1990.

Cleveland Cavaliers' First Championship: The Cleveland Cavaliers, led by LeBron James, won their first NBA championship in franchise history in the 2015-2016 season, overcoming a 3-1 deficit against the Golden State Warriors in the NBA Finals.

Sacramento Kings' Memorable Playoff Runs: The Sacramento Kings, particularly in the early 2000s, were known for their exciting brand of basketball and memorable playoff battles, including the controversial 2002 Western Conference Finals against the Los Angeles Lakers.

Toronto Raptors' Historic Title: The Toronto Raptors won their first NBA championship in the 2018-2019 season, becoming the first Canadian team to win an NBA title.

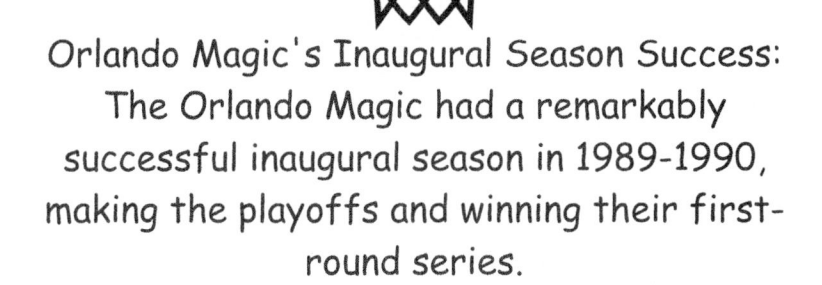

Orlando Magic's Inaugural Season Success: The Orlando Magic had a remarkably successful inaugural season in 1989-1990, making the playoffs and winning their first-round series.

Minnesota Timberwolves' Star Duo: The Minnesota Timberwolves featured the dynamic duo of Kevin Garnett and Stephon Marbury in the 1990s, showcasing two young stars with immense talent.

Charlotte Hornets' Expansion Success: The Charlotte Hornets, as an expansion team in the 1988-1989 season, exceeded expectations by making the playoffs in their second season.

Washington Wizards' Championship History: The Washington Wizards, formerly known as the Washington Bullets, won an NBA championship in 1978, led by Wes Unseld and Elvin Hayes.

Denver Nuggets' High-Scoring Games: The Denver Nuggets were known for their high-scoring games during the 1980s, including a memorable 186-184 triple-overtime victory over the Detroit Pistons in 1983, which remains the highest-scoring game in NBA history.

New Orleans Pelicans' Draft Lottery Luck: The New Orleans Pelicans won the NBA Draft Lottery in 2012 and selected Anthony Davis with the first overall pick, setting the stage for a new era in the franchise.

Memphis Grizzlies' "Grit and Grind" Era: The Memphis Grizzlies embraced a tough and physical style of play known as "Grit and Grind" during the 2010s, leading to multiple playoff appearances

Milwaukee Bucks' 20-Game Winning Streak: During the 1970-1971 season, the Milwaukee Bucks, led by Kareem Abdul-Jabbar and Oscar Robertson, went on a 20-game winning streak, the second-longest in NBA history at the time.

Houston Rockets' Back-to-Back Championships: The Houston Rockets won back-to-back NBA championships in the 1993-1994 and 1994-1995 seasons, led by Hakeem Olajuwon.

Indiana Pacers' Consistency: The Indiana Pacers made the playoffs for 21 consecutive seasons from 1989 to 2010, showcasing their long-term competitiveness.

Brooklyn Nets' Move to Brooklyn: The New Jersey Nets relocated to Brooklyn, New York, in 2012 and became the Brooklyn Nets, ushering in a new era for the franchise.

Phoenix Suns' Fastest Triple-Double: Devin Booker recorded the fastest triple-double in NBA history in 2021, achieving the feat in just 21 minutes and 14 seconds.

Utah Jazz's Iconic Home Court: The Utah Jazz have one of the most iconic home court advantages in the NBA, with their fans known for creating a raucous atmosphere at the Vivint Arena in Salt Lake City.

Dallas Mavericks' 2011 Playoff Run: The Dallas Mavericks' 2011 NBA championship run was marked by their resilience and ability to defeat favored opponents, including the Miami Heat in the NBA Finals.

Toronto Raptors' Record Win Streak: The Toronto Raptors had a franchise-record 15-game winning streak during the 2019-2020 season, setting a new team milestone.

Cleveland Cavaliers' NBA Finals Comeback: The Cleveland Cavaliers made a historic comeback in the 2016 NBA Finals, becoming the first team to rally from a 3-1 deficit to win the championship.

Los Angeles Clippers' Lob City Era: The Los Angeles Clippers' Lob City era, featuring stars like Chris Paul, Blake Griffin, and DeAndre Jordan, was known for its highlight-reel dunks and alley-oops.

Minnesota Timberwolves' First-Ever Draft Pick: The Minnesota Timberwolves selected Anthony Bennett with the first overall pick in the 2013 NBA Draft, marking their first-ever top overall pick.

Charlotte Hornets' Expansion Return: The Charlotte Hornets returned as an expansion team in 2004 after briefly relocating to New Orleans, restoring the historic franchise name.

Atlanta Hawks' Streak of Playoff Appearances: The Atlanta Hawks made the playoffs for 10 consecutive seasons from 2008 to 2017, marking a successful decade for the franchise.

Portland Trail Blazers' Iconic Guards: The Portland Trail Blazers have been home to legendary guards like Clyde Drexler and Damian Lillard, known for their scoring and leadership.

Miami Heat's "Big Three" Era: The Miami Heat formed a star-studded "Big Three" with LeBron James, Dwyane Wade, and Chris Bosh, leading to four consecutive NBA Finals appearances and two championships from 2010 to 2014.

New York Knicks' Iconic Madison Square Garden: The New York Knicks play their home games at Madison Square Garden, one of the most iconic and historic arenas in the world.

Denver Nuggets' Scoring Records: The Denver Nuggets are known for their high-scoring games and set a record for the most points scored by a team in a single game with 186 points in a triple-overtime game in 1983.

New Orleans Pelicans' Lottery Luck Again: The New Orleans Pelicans won the NBA Draft Lottery in 2019 and selected Zion Williamson with the first overall pick, securing another franchise-altering player.

Los Angeles Clippers' Recent Success: The Los Angeles Clippers have experienced a resurgence in recent years, becoming one of the top contenders in the Western Conference.

Boston Celtics' Iconic Parquet Floor: The Boston Celtics play their home games on the iconic parquet floor at TD Garden, a symbol of the team's storied history.

Indiana Pacers' Iconic Brawl: The Indiana Pacers were involved in a memorable brawl with the Detroit Pistons in 2004, known as the "Malice at the Palace," which led to significant suspensions and changes in league policies.

Toronto Raptors' First-Ever NBA Championship: The Toronto Raptors won their first NBA championship in 2019, making history as the first Canadian team to achieve this feat.

Philadelphia 76ers' Iconic Players: The Philadelphia 76ers have been home to legendary players like Julius Erving, known as "Dr. J," and Allen Iverson, who made a significant impact on the franchise's history.

Sacramento Kings' Move to Sacramento: The Sacramento Kings relocated from Kansas City to Sacramento in 1985, marking their debut in the California city.

Houston Rockets' Small-Ball Experiment: The Houston Rockets made headlines by adopting a small-ball lineup, emphasizing three-point shooting and versatility in recent seasons.

Utah Jazz's "Mailman" and "Stockton" Era: The Utah Jazz's dynamic duo of Karl Malone, known as "The Mailman," and John Stockton formed one of the most iconic partnerships in NBA history.

Memphis Grizzlies' "Grit and Grind" Legacy: The Memphis Grizzlies became known for their tough and physical style of play during the "Grit and Grind" era, making multiple playoff appearances.

San Antonio Spurs' International Influence: The San Antonio Spurs, under coach Gregg Popovich, embraced international talent and featured players like Tim Duncan (U.S. Virgin Islands), Manu Ginóbili (Argentina), and Tony Parker (France) in their championship-winning teams.

Golden State Warriors' "Strength in Numbers": The Golden State Warriors adopted the motto "Strength in Numbers" during their championship runs, emphasizing teamwork and depth.

Phoenix Suns' Seven Seconds or Less: The Phoenix Suns, led by coach Mike D'Antoni, popularized the "Seven Seconds or Less" offense, which prioritized fast-paced play and quick shot attempts.

Milwaukee Bucks' Kareem Abdul-Jabbar: Kareem Abdul-Jabbar, during his time with the Milwaukee Bucks, won three NBA MVP awards and led the team to an NBA championship in 1971.

Los Angeles Lakers' "Showtime" Era: The Los Angeles Lakers' "Showtime" era, led by Magic Johnson, was known for its fast-paced, high-scoring style of play and multiple championships in the 1980s.

Chicago Bulls' Dennis Rodman: Dennis Rodman, known for his colorful personality and rebounding prowess, played a pivotal role in the Chicago Bulls' second three-peat of championships in the 1990s.

Dallas Mavericks' Dirk Nowitzki: Dirk Nowitzki, one of the greatest power forwards in NBA history, spent his entire career with the Dallas Mavericks, leading them to their first NBA championship in 2011.

Miami Heat's Iconic White Hot Uniforms: The Miami Heat's "White Hot" uniforms became iconic during the LeBron James era, symbolizing the team's playoff intensity and success.

Sacramento Kings' Notable Playoff Rivalries: The Sacramento Kings had intense playoff rivalries with teams like the Los Angeles Lakers and Dallas Mavericks during the early 2000s.

Cleveland Cavaliers' First NBA Finals Appearance: The Cleveland Cavaliers made their first-ever NBA Finals appearance in 2007, led by LeBron James.

Portland Trail Blazers' Iconic "Rip City" Phrase: The phrase "Rip City" became synonymous with the Portland Trail Blazers, coined by announcer Bill Schonely during a game in 1971.

New York Knicks' Iconic Players: The New York Knicks have been home to legendary players like Willis Reed, Charles Oakley, and Patrick Ewing, who left an indelible mark on the franchise.

Detroit Pistons' "Bad Boys" Defense: The Detroit Pistons' "Bad Boys" teams of the late 1980s were known for their tenacious defense, led by players like Isiah Thomas and Dennis Rodman.

Minnesota Timberwolves' Kevin Garnett: Kevin Garnett, a franchise icon, spent the majority of his career with the Minnesota Timberwolves and won the NBA MVP award in 2004.

Toronto Raptors' "We The North" Campaign: The Toronto Raptors' "We The North" campaign became a rallying cry for the team and its passionate fan base during their championship run in 2019.

Orlando Magic's Inaugural Season Success: The Orlando Magic, an expansion team in 1989, made the playoffs in their inaugural season, an unusual achievement for a new franchise.

Washington Wizards' "Bullets" Era: The Washington Wizards were originally known as the Washington Bullets and won their only NBA championship in 1978 under that name.

Los Angeles Clippers' Iconic Dunkers: The Los Angeles Clippers have featured some of the NBA's most iconic dunkers, including Blake Griffin and DeAndre Jordan, known for their high-flying plays.

Golden State Warriors' Splash Brothers: The Golden State Warriors became known for their "Splash Brothers," Stephen Curry and Klay Thompson, who redefined three-point shooting in the NBA.

New Orleans Pelicans' Drafting Anthony Davis: The New Orleans Pelicans won the NBA Draft Lottery in 2012 and selected Anthony Davis with the first overall pick, leading to a transformative era for the franchise.

Utah Jazz's John Stockton and Karl Malone: John Stockton and Karl Malone, both Hall of Famers, formed one of the most prolific duos in NBA history while playing for the Utah Jazz.

Charlotte Hornets' Return to Buzz City: The Charlotte Hornets, previously the Charlotte Bobcats, reclaimed their historic name, the Charlotte Hornets, in 2014, restoring a beloved franchise identity.

Indiana Pacers' Reggie Miller: Reggie Miller, a legendary Pacers player, was known for his clutch three-point shooting and memorable playoff battles, particularly against the New York Knicks.

Phoenix Suns' Legendary "The Shot" by Gar Heard: In Game 5 of the 1976 NBA Finals, Gar Heard hit a dramatic shot known as "The Shot" to send the game into triple overtime, a historic moment in NBA Finals history.

Denver Nuggets' High-Scoring Teams: The Denver Nuggets have consistently been among the highest-scoring teams in NBA history, with several seasons averaging over 120 points per game.

Toronto Raptors' Jurassic Park: During the Toronto Raptors' playoff runs, fans gathered in "Jurassic Park" outside Scotiabank Arena to support their team, creating an electric atmosphere.

Cleveland Cavaliers' "The Block, The Shot, The Stop": LeBron James' famous block, Kyrie Irving's clutch three-pointer, and the Cavaliers' defensive stop secured their historic comeback in the 2016 NBA Finals.

Sacramento Kings' "Miracle on 33rd Street": In 1989, the Sacramento Kings orchestrated a dramatic comeback known as the "Miracle on 33rd Street" against the Los Angeles Lakers, winning after trailing by 35 points.

Chicago Bulls' Iconic Introduction Music: The Chicago Bulls are known for their iconic introduction music, "Sirius" by The Alan Parsons Project, which sets the stage for the team's entrance.

San Antonio Spurs' "Big Three" Era: The San Antonio Spurs' "Big Three" of Tim Duncan, Manu Ginóbili, and Tony Parker led the team to multiple championships and became synonymous with the franchise's success.

Golden State Warriors' Historic 73-Win Season: In the 2015-2016 season, the Golden State Warriors set an NBA record with 73 regular-season wins, surpassing the previous record held by the 1995-1996 Chicago Bulls.

Boston Celtics' Bill Russell's Championships: Bill Russell, a Celtics legend, won an astonishing 11 NBA championships during his illustrious career, the most by any player in NBA history.

Chicago Bulls' 72-10 Record: The 1995-1996 Chicago Bulls, led by Michael Jordan, set a record by finishing the regular season with a 72-10 win-loss record, which stood as the best regular-season record until 2016.

Los Angeles Lakers' Kobe Bryant's Farewell Game: Kobe Bryant's farewell game in 2016 was a remarkable moment in NBA history, as he scored 60 points in his final game as a Los Angeles Laker.

Milwaukee Bucks' Kareem Abdul-Jabbar's Scoring Titles: Kareem Abdul-Jabbar, during his time with the Milwaukee Bucks and later the Lakers, won six NBA scoring titles, showcasing his offensive prowess.

Los Angeles Clippers' Lob City Dunkers: The Los Angeles Clippers, during the "Lob City" era, featured numerous high-flying dunkers, including DeAndre Jordan, Blake Griffin, and Chris Paul.

Toronto Raptors' Jurassic Park Viewing Parties: Raptors fans gather outside Scotiabank Arena during the playoffs for "Jurassic Park" viewing parties, creating a unique and passionate atmosphere.

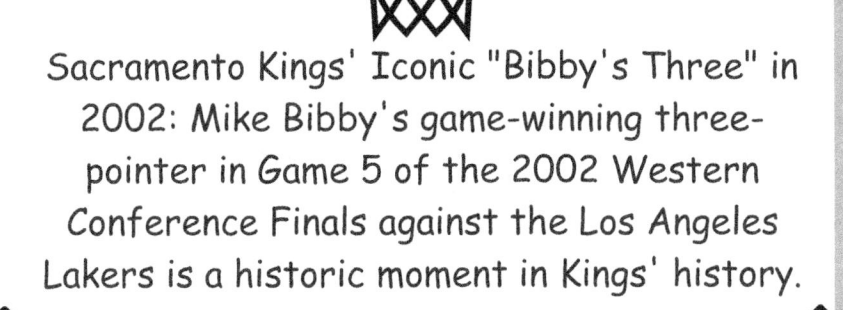

Sacramento Kings' Iconic "Bibby's Three" in 2002: Mike Bibby's game-winning three-pointer in Game 5 of the 2002 Western Conference Finals against the Los Angeles Lakers is a historic moment in Kings' history.

Houston Rockets' Clutch City: The Houston Rockets, known as "Clutch City," won back-to-back NBA championships in 1994 and 1995, showcasing their ability to perform under pressure.

Philadelphia 76ers' Iconic "Process" Era: The "Trust the Process" era in Philadelphia emphasized rebuilding through the draft, leading to the acquisition of star players like Joel Embiid and Ben Simmons.

Portland Trail Blazers' Iconic "Rip City" Cheer: The phrase "Rip City," coined by broadcaster Bill Schonely in the 1970s, remains an iconic cheer for Trail Blazers fans.

Printed in Great Britain
by Amazon